Alfred's
INSTRUMENTAL
CD+ INSIDE
PLAY-ALONG

Tenor Saxophone

Level 2–3

HIT MOVIE & TV
INSTRUMENTAL SOLOS

Songs and themes from the latest movies and television shows

Arranged by Bill Galliford and Ethan Neuburg

Recordings produced by Dan Warner, Doug Emery, and Lee Levin

Contents

D1088488

CITY OF STARS
(from *La La Land*)

Music by JUSTIN HURWITZ
Lyrics by BENJ PASEK & JUSTIN PAUL

City of Stars - 2 - 1

3

City of Stars - 2 - 2

ANOTHER DAY OF SUN

(from *La La Land*)

Track 4: Demo
Track 5: Play-Along

Music by JUSTIN HURWITZ
Lyrics by BENJ PASEK & JUSTIN PAUL

Another Day of Sun - 2 - 1

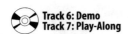
Track 6: Demo
Track 7: Play-Along

MIA & SEBASTIAN'S THEME

(from *La La Land*)

Music by
JUSTIN HURWITZ

Track 8: Demo
Track 9: Play-Along

A MAN AND HIS BEASTS

(from *Fantastic Beasts and Where to Find Them*)

Composed by
JAMES NEWTON HOWARD

A Man and His Beasts - 3 - 1

NEWT SAYS GOODBYE TO TINA/
JACOB'S BAKERY

(from *Fantastic Beasts and Where to Find Them*)

Track 10: Demo
Track 11: Play-Along

Composed by
JAMES NEWTON HOWARD

Tenderly, with expression (♩ = 48)
"Newt Says Goodbye to Tina"

Newt Says Goodbye to Tina/Jacob's Bakery - 2 - 1

11

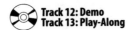

Track 12: Demo
Track 13: Play-Along

KOWALSKI RAG

(from *Fantastic Beasts and Where to Find Them*)

Composed by
JAMES NEWTON HOWARD

Kowalski Rag - 2 - 1

Track 14: Demo
Track 15: Play-Along

HEATHENS
(from *Suicide Squad*)

Words and Music by
TYLER JOSEPH

Heathens - 2 - 1

GHOSTBUSTERS

Track 16: Demo
Track 17: Play-Along

Words and Music by
RAY PARKER, JR.

Ghostbusters - 2 - 1

Track 18: Demo
Track 19: Play-Along

From The LEGO® Movie
EVERYTHING IS AWESOME

Written by
SHAWN PATTERSON

Everything Is Awesome - 2 - 1

Track 20: Demo
Track 21: Play-Along

RUNNIN' HOME TO YOU
(from the television series *The Flash*)

Words & Music by
BENJ PASEK & JUSTIN PAUL
Arranged by BLAKE NEELY

Runnin' Home to You - 2 - 1

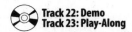

Track 22: Demo
Track 23: Play-Along

BEAUTY AND THE BEAST
(from Walt Disney's *Beauty and the Beast*)

Lyrics by
HOWARD ASHMAN

Music by
ALAN MENKEN

Beauty and the Beast - 2 - 1

Track 24: Demo
Track 25: Play-Along

AMAZONS OF THEMYSCIRA
(Main Theme from *Wonder Woman*)

Composed by
RUPERT GREGSON-WILLIAMS

WESTWORLD: OPENING THEME

Track 26: Demo
Track 27: Play-Along

By RAMIN DJAWADI

With stealth (♩. = 74)

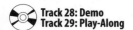

Track 28: Demo
Track 29: Play-Along

JUST LIKE FIRE
(from *Alice Through the Looking Glass*)

Words and Music by
OSCAR HOLTER, MAX MARTIN,
SHELLBACK and ALECIA MOORE

Moderate rock (♩ = 82)

PARTS OF A TENOR SAXOPHONE
AND FINGERING CHART

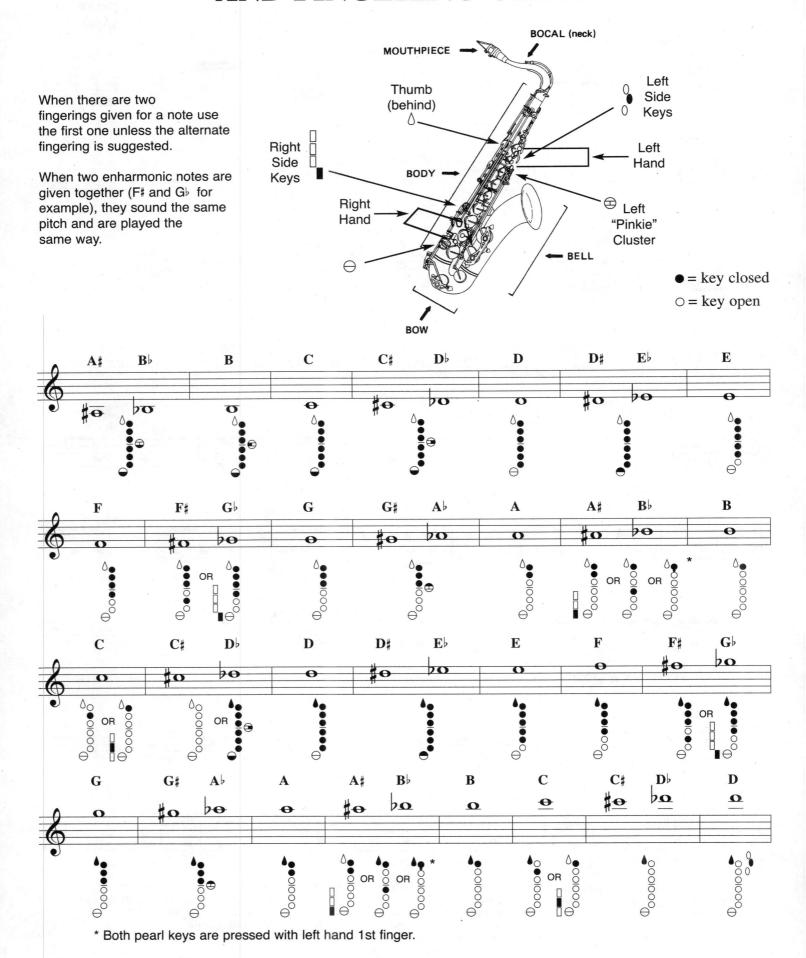

* Both pearl keys are pressed with left hand 1st finger.